SOME CLEAR SOUVENIR

E. Tracy Grinnell

O BOOKS
2006

I GRATEFULLY ACKNOWLEDGE the editors of the following publications where poems and excerpts have been previously published, mostly in earlier versions: *Conundrum, Downtown Brooklyn, Estuaire* (trans. Daniel Canty), *The New Review of Literature, Primary Writing, Ribot, 26,* and *Washington Square.*

THIS MANUSCRIPT OWES MUCH to the work of Nicole Brossard (*Surfaces of Sense*), Danielle Collobert (*It Then*), Jean Daive (*A Lesson in Music*), Alberto Giacometti ("A Figure in a Box Between Two Boxes Which Are Houses"), and Giorgio Agamben (*The Coming Community*) in addition to works cited in epigraphs.

I OFFER MANY WARM THANKS to Leslie Scalapino and Craig Watson for their close readings and generous feedback, to Keith and Rosmarie Waldrop, and also to Rachel Bers, Paul Foster Johnson and Mark Tardi for their kind support along the way.

ISBN # 1-882022-59-9   PRICE $12.00

Cover design by E. Tracy Grinnell in collaboration with Leslie Scalapino and Amy Evans McClure

Cover photographs: "Feathers, Bird, Sword, Drape" by Claude Cahun. Reprinted with permission from The Jersey Heritage Trust. "Pigeons" by Ed Silver. Reprinted with the artist's permission. "Trees & sky," found image. Artist unknown.

Book design by Amy Evans McClure

*Think of the edge of the city, and the traffic there. Some
clear souvenir—A photograph. (A newspaper clipping
caught in the frame of the mirror).*

—JASPER JOHNS, Jasper Johns: Work Since 1974

Clip 1

one
figure
in
hand
to
scale
or
outside
the
body
blown
into

hollow
graphic
into
pieces
into
shifts
what
is
reflected
or
reflecting
over
sight
over
sound
again
diminishing
surfaces
form
against
this

medium
tracing
and
or
this
one
in
hand

coming
apart

Clip 2

a rooftop has an enemy

an owl

a cone of confusion

scansion of acoustics

or before sound

a crematorium

visually unresolved

(before)   remains

leaves that only look

like the birds

between them

physiology limits
visual memory

ash or   bodies
in glass

example

delineation out of time   some cartography
of movement as though sentences   speaking
sentences underwater
some sentences
in the first sense, second person. the swell
the broken time. a sentence in mind
the space around the body's

in taking leave of its thought

Clip 3

moments   coming

as isolate ringing

in a glass cube one hand

unsure of being external or

internal to the dimensions or

definitions

my hands in relation

another's handling of them

what they are capable of

or incapable

definitions

bodily harm or other harm

to come *to*

without physical contact or

definition

I can't isolate

the glass cube

from the ether

example

expression of the body towards anything
at times one stands still, this goes on
static and plastic:
                        the horizon the body
stands for
the horizon   is stationary
in tidewater

any place
other than itself   remains

anything   anywhere   in the dust

Clip 4

so I am slowly   to gather
the sense   what was
a figure

to gather
what epics

I will   evidently

a euphemism

a flag
for example

is not a reflection
flies *against*

a place for tombs

neither gray expanse

nor ground cover

nothing returns

only
accumulates

example

days: night and day

herein lie the absences: to have forgotten what
it is to resist, what we were before now where

there is birth, the war, a day
resistance   a sentence   a day

a night, a difference, no difference   absence is
resolute

rupture is
rapture

Clip 5

pigeons at four o'clock

a dream about bow ties
flying

my former residence

frustrated, ceaseless

haunting the ghost

is not yet dead

or yet

the residual of a sleeping dream

the residual of dismantled similarities, a waking one

is this

a figure
at four o'clock

the war, but more deliberate
silence

is not the swarm
that calms the agitation

of four hands or disembodied

motivation that is external

to motion so that one haunts

or is haunted by the actual world:

example

the emotive affliction of certain
explanations   —11

elision for *pale in comparison*

or how when there is wind there cannot be
other things

stone complicates
the sand   physical emergence
dispersed   along a shore
lined with
it is the same with
pronouns

example

not geography, the body
first, then battlegrounds

interference   and fragment

          that lists
          forget

                    that love,
like pronouns
          divides its questions:

atmospheric, secular
argumentative

                    that a bird *un*hovers

or perhaps a swallow understands the intimacy
of sentences

                    to fulfill
                    to diagram, or retrieve

Clip 6

a skyline of windows become ideology, what is
left
to catch
in open nets

                  some fragments   save
                  us

a line or delineation *towards*
there for
what our bodies are
in time

against what our definitions
are

in qualified space

fallen into cones instead, for sight
proportion, alarm

example

one skyline
shrinks my sky
by day

over-exposed
by night   against
against seeing
bodies   as there

the shadow
that displaces

its own shadow
divided

when historically
referencing

inhabited, isolate
self

was nothing
flying

save flags

Clip 7

blind

wind

or the reverse
fingerprint

in newsprint

is the absence
    of my shadow   caught in mirrors

human body-blind
to environment
                gesture-line

crystalline airborne
                figure

a fugue

empty of organs

what tears
about
the body

wind

blind

—15

Clip 8

form, first form
no first
place

spans of time that form
first marked

      indelible   by loss

continual marking
windows fly
let apart

    sound out
phonemes before

questions

undress, ceaseless outside

depart

example

the distance

between the figurative landscape

and another   figurative body

exploration that is no longer theoretical
                  is various   patchwork
internal

framed away   in time

violent   a mechanism
violence

of this   one

remains discontinuous
or lucid   already

as element

Clip 9

cartographic medium

between graphite and obituary

what if devoid of imperial
potentials

lines are drawn

and redrawn

rituals

of the body

the psyche

from
my
window

the field

light redraws
against

an indescribable
order

imposed   a tattoo

recovers

the scar

example

when I thought I felt

something

it was only

that a moment submerged

in water is the same

as another

or the difference between

touching external surfaces—a wall, a stranger's coatsleeve

how I do this

and land, fragmentary, in night

my night

its seams

my night

—19

example

a brush   with death
walking a dreamscape

brushed against

            this time   of absence
when described collapses
a visual scape

      what otherwise emerges

        (call it something else)

       listing   itself
            (escape)

delays   newer   things
only discontinuous
sequence

          (closer   ever)

Clip 10

how this time is a fact of shared space
looking to pass through, undifferentiated
memory always has a back door

       no one word settles
       me

or rather than resist
rather than resolution

such that lists

fall from

one

how I gathered words as clusters for memory. how I am therefore enclosed. how the images of those memories in daylight cast against the combinations of associations. how real or imagined it was real. how the collapse of images bends time. how the actual event, and how the trace of an image. how when there is no longer any argument there is only element

example

how time thinks

is out of time   human-blind

under water   suspension

sensate refraction   when flocking

          versions of flight   from the usual

blinds come down

or why there is still light
enough

I am

in the first place

is out of time

in the first place

time alights

Clip 11

visually unresolved

as the other side
of an argument

matter
of minutes

ignoring the bell, the blow

such that it always matters

erasable lines, out lines

train windows repeat

as flags, a thought

caught in the

first mirror

lastly

example

the frames

of captive
relations

through a door, trap door

to the flatlands
          leveled

instead of an alphabet

I try
to feel
against
the elements

small grave
smaller example

the remains resolve

instead of an army

frame
of my
mirror

beside or beyond

(above)

the surface

Clip 12

an imprint

   among features, figures

    along the surface-line
    in order to follow
    what was

  a premonition

     a glance
     only

example

after the pronominal

sentence

      subjects

         stop looking

     to words

or looking to

sequence, of states

this sequence for borders
then rupture

of landscape, borders for desire

of borders, a photographic

stand for sequence
therefore

borders for nothing
and sequence

      therefore dreamscape

      only sequence
of faces
out of the blur

        these languages therefore

regions   amid language

example

found in one
state

of not looking
          in the habit of another

forced back

untouchable mark
residual mark
future

                    shadow
instinct towards
antagonism
when out of
order

I circle

outside of lines
change ringing
lines

around one
figure, an utterance

hovers inside

          the field

Clip 13

my interior surrounds me

then impossibility, being such

a troubled boundary

beyond is what comes to

matter for choice

is matter, such as it is

      fields made of it, in the image

example

here, in remembering

things done, undone, not yet
done   the erasure

        the dream apart
        from the day
        original
        day

hammered ground
hollowed out

to hold
the sound

        and let up
        the sea

        it faces

Clip 14

memory
  somewhere else

figure a body
projects a figure   the body

      declining into
an actual background

of stone—marble, granite, lime—

the figure, lines in a field
a photographic

flash, of intimacy

        in moments of comparison

in words, before
  when time was   credible
        the body was

the place remains something else, not a place
relative to internal geography

something escapes
not by violence

    by giving way, by calling it
    something else

example

this is not a pane of glass

though I am politically

determined

inside of something

—33

Clip 16

cold material

of first
flight

the night
everywhere

I didn't yet
know

the owl
around
me

for
the heart
of my
thief

clearer even
then

on the back
of a massacre

whether fist or alignment

for a life-long
life

Clip 17

the street that lies
under snow

complacency grows
against itself

passive lights
                    along the bridge, the city

            against the city, blown away
            impure, reactive

the seed of thought   that lists

                    wakes up the street

            periodic

example

hovering into
the grain, what already has to be

      against
      the same space

I am alone in the atmosphere
a rooftop tropic

owls against
the moon

what is already outside
my window, time

             as if to look, an empty sound

               from the remains
               a repetition

recorded on
different pages or

in different books

Clip 18

tending to become opposite
in decline

to make this
        fractal eclipse

a way of clarity
        masks of birds

                of walls and walls of birds, leaf formations

having nothing
to do with visually catching

        the differences
        between the grain

                of resolution, the grain
                of silver silos, girders
                of steel and bone

example

no rooftop
canopy under
which I lie awake

in ground cover
a *cone of confusion*

while water
erodes   in water

visions of windows blur

windows become plastic

awake
and are
blinded

it could very well mean nothing
(except that I lie awake

unable to name it)

that on certain occasions I pretend
it does not exist

example

each tautology through an account
of it, each location
                        as it was

figuring an algebra of emotion, for each case
after the planetary sense
of relations
                    in real time

        to mark planetary alignments

        with a fist

Clip 19

how each lover is
a composite
of lovers, a temporal
proximity

to fell
as if a state, a landscape

an island
off the coast

the glass cube, undifferentiated other
out of time

      recurrence as so much
            algebra

the determination
of wings

      the same sentence
accelerated to silence so

many figures
fall

example

       this and or
this then

broken surface, tensile mirage   listing til
                        it severed glass

     each fleeing

     not after thought

caught or
catching   word for word

       needs element   more anything, anywhere   as in

case
in diminishing
point

       after collapsing view
          in strobe

     images eddy

         lucent
         as
             souvenir

Clip 20

the shifting scale

for the medium in hand

for having had

before

the land and dream, the scope

in steps taken, escape

figured   a *figure*

in a box

in danger or miniature

blown apart or *between*

two boxes a body

finds itself between

two houses, which are hands

which are houses

my hands and the illusion of falling

my hand has the illusion of falling

Clip 21

a skull drawn
in the sand
to mark

this figure

      placed lengthwise on a map

between
impossibility or

          linguistic
          possession

bedfellows in the field
of vision, the other sense
of the inevitable

                what otherwise emerges

      that the residual
      language is physical

                fervent   dark

example

each question in question
or in parts, each negation
where you

confuses the intention

I have no dreams or ambitions

in this section of the city

this train an arboretum

I am on

I can never think

amid the cemetery

I have no dreams or ambitions
I have only this quarter
of an hour

as the blue daylight

is no longer a filter

for the violet of response

I love when you say   *no*

example

that one trades notions
of discontent

for other forms
of it, for words traded in
                their own condition

        the progression toward nothing
                that this is a true discussion

where the residual is sense
in other forms

Clip 22

the light
on impulse
shapes

oppositional
microscopic
forces

the seasons
refusing to change

the oceans are only

gravity demonstrative

afternoon in pieces

on the floor

to reckon with

the same as *to love*

from the inside of escape, of something that
has been renamed before

          violet light, violent
          night

example

yellow structure
close to the bridge
a reflection of color
or proximity

world goes gray
no sky

newsprint gray
of everything
changes everything

the world
in a lover away
in the world

to still go on, enumerating
things

Clip 23

catching in
weathered fabric
of the distant water

while weightless

on a plane, in a place
giving way

analogy
to mourning

      facing, effacing

the only material

          in words

a relation

    of hands

or sound

    of fabric
      relenting

example

space remains

the membrane

of wind
    against   surfaces

figures of bodies

trace

against time
then fall

after listing, careening

against

premonition

sequence

Clip 24

among the graves

marked *guest*

        of houses   of wanderers
scattered in light

this afternoon is the same time
every afternoon

to pass through again

myself tomorrow

will seem

        the same as yesterday's

perfect hour

to pass

to name
but everyone's

houses

shuddering

under flags

remain between
gestures

all things
in form
in faces

Clip 25

      call out the cities

                          are ruins

            by repeated
            location

because I think
of things

a false allegiance

        of unlocatable repetitions

homing in
those eyes

the ruins

in the contrary
        shade

  my allegiances
are too great

            I am left
              anonymous
              there

example

the physical relations

for eyes

to see   though
              dismantled measures

                        and lists
                        of things

seem as seas

              this was the future

              to find
              the inclusive
              among them

      unboundaried

                  seeing parts
                        arranged

            in fugues
                  to weather

Clip 26

gatherers and
wanderers, a swarm

       thinking
       we are
       surrounding

then
verging
lines
a horizon   particular to
                       homing

      wings beating
        rooftop

 the smaller catastrophe

 of body

 of necessity

      another face

         and sphere

  while
  in fear

example

on one window a habit
of expression

      before I lay down
      to close my eyes

of projection

             where transparencies
                 alter the view

    of reaction

             when one
             is framed
             by another

             a prism   of views

and then, this habit of seeing
things
             through windows

example

identification of *elsewhere*

is hope
a geography

of possibility
gathered or lost   among the same
to seem

for the sea
to many

the wind forms

changelings

Clip 27

that the illusion
of falling

is the illusion, element and something else
body-like

to figure   the pages
are versions, which are houses

or records of naming
which are diaries

of bodies, which are life-like

are shifting between
something figured
ingrained

into element, some image
absent from time

after the facts, some constant
residua

some clear souvenir

Clip 28

time is nowhere

    but to distinguish
the absolute from
the variable

forms of calling
names, cities
sentences

await
the demands
of pages

or hybrid inside
of something
alate

            deeper in the indifferent
            structure

the wings
alone

example

seasons or
months   *july* intransitive

       or the way things diminish

          as a form
             of repetition

    when the way
    they accumulate

     presupposes
     language amid   difference

out of the blur

drawn into

   phases of quietism
facing or passing

       for the longest time

Clip 29

false life

made of categories

actual body

made of records

false memory

made of afterimages

actual records

made of sensory events

false images

made of actual violence

actual life

made of questions

false categories

made of actual infringements

actual words

made of false surfaces

false questions made of words

in actual arrangement

example

falling
out
vision
floor
upon
field
verge
of
an
image
first
windows
for
time
and
inalienable
light
inalienable
line

distinct
realm
of
confusable
things

in
space
or
different
resolution
collapse
of
various

imagery
leaves
imagery
to
the
wolves

Clip 30

the forward and reverse
motion

      of mathematical
      loves

          the habits of each version
          of recollection

             strangers are no more than
             locations
               in a temporal field

each utterance
acceptance
      or denial

      what presence
      my hand has
      in a field

           of pigeons
           or wolves

    what quietude
    raises questions

      what borders
        or lists to keep

      and keep

example

how I revisited a location from the past, and how this location came to be revised in the present. how the clarity of argument is the remainder of desire. how desire is not subversive, but the remainder. how the body escapes. how this created in me a failure to communicate. how this failure to communicate led me to recognize lovers in the faces of strangers. how these faces were mirrors, refractions of events onto the structures around them. how collapse seems inevitable. decay takes on mantles of emotional projection. how I surrender to noise and decay among abstract locations. these locations are history

example

this
and
or
this
then

sentences trace
the figure
which traces
the body   collapses
the order
                which lists forget

the sequence, unresolved
figure in space
the field or
sense
        of space

                against time, it fell
                        so far
                            it severed glass
                                to grain
the periodic
graphic
the body does   continuous sequence   the body in the organ
  in the body of the

blur and
or

this is a sentence

and this is.

and this is

Other *O BOOKS*

www.obooks.com ◆ 5729 Clover Drive, Oakland CA 94618

Distributed by Small Press Distribution, 1341 Seventh Street, Berkeley CA 94710

Towards The Primeval Lightning Field, Will Alexander, $12.00

Return of the World, Todd Baron, $10.00

A Certain Slant of Sunlight, Ted Berrigan, $12.00

Mob, Abigail Child, $12.00

CYMK, Michael Coffey, $14.00

Moira, Norma Cole, $12.00

It Then, Danielle Collobert, $10.00

Lapses, John Crouse, $10.00

Headlines, John Crouse, $12.00

The Arcades, Michael Davidson, $12.00

Candor, Alan Davies, $10.00

iduna, kari edwards, $12.00

Rome, A Mobile Home, Jerry Estrin, Roof Books and Potes & Poets with
O Books, $9.00

Turn Left in Order to Go Right, Norman Fischer, $12.00

Time Rations, Benjamin Friedlander, $12.00

Startle Response, Heather Fuller, $12.00

byt, William Fuller, $12.00

The Sugar Borders, William Fuller, $12.00

War and Peace 2, editors Judith Goldman and Leslie Scalapino, $14.00

DeathStar/rico-chet, Judith Goldman, $14.00

Phantom Anthems, Robert Grenier, $12.00

What I Believe Transpiration/Transpiring Minnesota, Robert Grenier,
$24.00

The Inveterate Life, Jessica Grim, $12.00

Fray, Jessica Grim, $12.00

Music or Forgetting, E. Tracy Grinnell, $12.00

Memory Play, Carla Harryman, $9.00

The Words/after Carl Sandburg's Rootabaga Stories and Jean-Paul Sartre,
Carla Harryman, $12.00

The Quietist, Fanny Howe, $9.00

Around Sea, Brenda Iijima, $12.00

VEL, P. Inman, $12.00

60 lv bo(e)mbs, Paolo Javier, $12.00

The History of the Loma People, Paul D. Korvah, $12.00

248 mgs., a panic picnic, Susan Landers, $12.00

Curve, Andrew Levy, $12.00

Values Chauffeur You, Andrew Levy, $12.00

Dreaming Close By, Rick London, $12.00

Abjections, Rick London, $5.00

Dissuasion Crowds the Slow Worker, Lori Lubeski, $10.00

Plum Stones / Cartoons of No Heaven, Michael McClure, $13.00

The Case, Laura Moriarty, $12.00

Home on the Range (The Night Sky with Stars in My Mouth), Tenney
  Nathanson, $12.00

Criteria, Sianne Ngai, $11.00

Close to me & Closer . . . (The Language of Heaven) and Désamère,
  Alice Notley, $12.00

Catenary Odes, Ted Pearson, $12.00

Collision Center, Randall Potts, $12.00

Light, Jerry Ratch, $12.00

(where late the sweet) BIRDS SANG, Stephen Ratcliffe, $12.00

Tottering State, Tom Raworth, $15.00

Kismet, Pat Reed, $12.00

Cold Heaven, Camille Roy, $12.00

The Seven Voices, Lisa Samuels, $12.00

Crowd and not evening or light, Leslie Scalapino, $12.00

Enough, an anthology edited by Leslie Scalapino and Rick London, $16.00

O ONE/AN ANTHOLOGY, ed. Leslie Scalapino, $12.00

O TWO/AN ANTHOLOGY: What is the inside, what is outside?, ed. Leslie
  Scalapino, $12.00

O/4: Subliminal Time, ed. Leslie Scalapino, $12.00

War and Peace, ed. Leslie Scalapino, $14.00

The India Book: Essays and Translations, Andrew Schelling, $12.00

". . . But I Couldn't Speak . . .", Jono Schneider, $12.00

Rumors of Buildings To Live In, Keith Shein, $12.00

A's Dream, Aaron Shurin, $12.00

Partisans, Rodrigo Toscano, $12.00

Lilyfoil, Elizabeth Treadwell, $12.00

Trespasses, Padcha Tuntha-obas, $12.00

Homing Devices, Liz Waldner, $12.00

Picture of The Picture of The Image in The Glass, Craig Watson, $12.00